HAITI

TRUDY J. HANMER

HAITI

Franklin Watts
New York/London/Toronto/Sydney/1988
A First Book

Map by Vantage Art

Photographs courtesy of: Photo Researchers, Inc.: pp. 18, 26, 35
& 39 (Odette Mennesson-Rigaud), 31 (Margot Granitsas), 67 (Fritz
Henle); United Nations: pp. 20 (Philip Teuscher), 23 (J. Viesti),
27; Culver Pictures, Inc.: pp. 43, 49; The Bettmann
Archive, Inc.: pp. 56, 58, 61, 78; UPI/Bettmann Newsphotos: pp. 85, 88.

Library of Congress Cataloging-in-Publication Data

Hanmer, Trudy J.
Haiti / Trudy J. Hanmer.
p.   cm.—(A First book)
Includes index.
Summary: Discusses the history of Haiti, its struggle for
independence, and its economy, culture, arts, religion, and people.
ISBN 0-531-10479-6
1. Haiti—Juvenile literature.   [1. Haiti.]   I. Title.
E1915.2.H36   1988

972.94—dc19   87-16483
                                                        CIP
                                                         AC

CONTENTS

For Matt

HAITI

INTRODUCTION

In the middle of the night of February 6, 1986, a U.S. Air Force C-141 transport plane landed at François Duvalier Airport outside Port-au-Prince, Haiti's capital city. Across that city at almost the same moment, a heavily guarded motorcade left for the airport. The passengers in the automobiles included Haiti's President, Jean-Claude Duvalier, popularly known as "Baby Doc"; his wife, Michele; their infant daughter; and nearly two dozen relatives and friends.

These people were fleeing a revolution in Haiti. They feared that they would be imprisoned or murdered if they stayed. As they sped through the gates of the palace, many of them realized that this might be their last view of the magnificent, gleaming-white presidential headquarters. For nearly three decades the Duvalier family had lived in wealth and luxury there and had ruled Haiti through an absolute dictatorship. Most Haitians now believed that the country had not profited from their rule.

The C-141 headed for France, Haiti's "mother country." France had promised Baby Doc and his entourage temporary asylum.

The Haitian dictator left behind a bitter legacy. Haiti is the poorest nation in the Western Hemisphere. Nearly 90 percent of all Haitians live a peasant existence of grinding poverty, malnutrition, disease, and unemployment. Less than one-fifth of Haitian people can read and write, and in 1980 the life expectancy of the average Haitian was forty-five. Haiti is severely overcrowded. The nation's population grows at a rate of approximately 2 percent per year; in the countryside every arable acre is crowded with people.

One million people live in the capital city of Port-au-Prince. Seventy percent of them live in desperate slum conditions. They have no running water, no sewage system, no electricity, and no garbage removal. Small black children with orange hair are a common sight; their unusual appearance results from kwashiorkor, a protein-deficiency disease. During the rainy season the slums are even worse. Torrential downpours flood the slums, contributing to disease and often drowning the slums' weaker inhabitants.

Yet Port-au-Prince continues to grow as landless people from the countryside flock to the city in search of work. The 50 percent unemployment rate does not discourage them. The population of the city grew at a rate of ten thousand a year throughout the 1960s; it tripled between 1975 and 1980. This great population growth has occurred during a time when thousands of Haitians escaped their country—most to the United States, many as illegal aliens.

The plight of modern Haiti is particularly tragic because Haiti —known in the past as Saint-Domingue—was once the richest piece of land per acre in the Western Hemisphere. Eighteenth-century Europeans nicknamed the island the "Eden of the Western World." Haitian sugar, coffee, and indigo plantations earned great riches for their owners. The major powers of Europe tried desperately to wrest control of this prize possession from France.

In spite of the colony's prosperity, all was not well in Saint-Domingue. Underlying its wealth were dictatorships even more hateful than those of any of the modern Haitian rulers. The success and riches of the colony of Haiti rested on the backs of the island's slave labor. Ninety percent of the island's population during its period of greatest wealth were black people who lived under the harshest form of slavery.

Modern Haiti is an incredibly poor nation. It was born from the ashes of one of the wealthiest and most evil societies of colonial times. Yet Haiti is a land of color, of drama, of comedy, and of tragedy. To understand Haiti today it is necessary to look at the people and the land, and at the forces of history that have influenced both.

CHAPTER ONE

"DAUGHTER OF AFRICA"

There are thousands of islands in the Caribbean Sea, but only fifty or so are inhabited. Haiti occupies the western third of the large island of Hispaniola, situated in the Caribbean between Cuba and Puerto Rico, 600 miles (966 km) from the coast of Florida. Hispaniola is one of four islands making up the Greater Antilles. Haiti's shape has been compared to a crab's claw whose pincers are aimed west toward its Cuban neighbors. But it is the Dominican Republic—the nation that occupies the eastern two-thirds of Hispaniola—that has most often attracted the attention of its neighbor, Haiti. Haiti and the Dominican Republic have shared the island uneasily for three hundred years. Haiti covers nearly 11,000 square miles (28,500 sq km). The nation includes three offshore islands—Gonâve, Tortué, and Vache.

The Land

Haiti is a mountainous land. In fact, the word *Haiti*, given to the nation as a name at the time of its independence in 1804, is

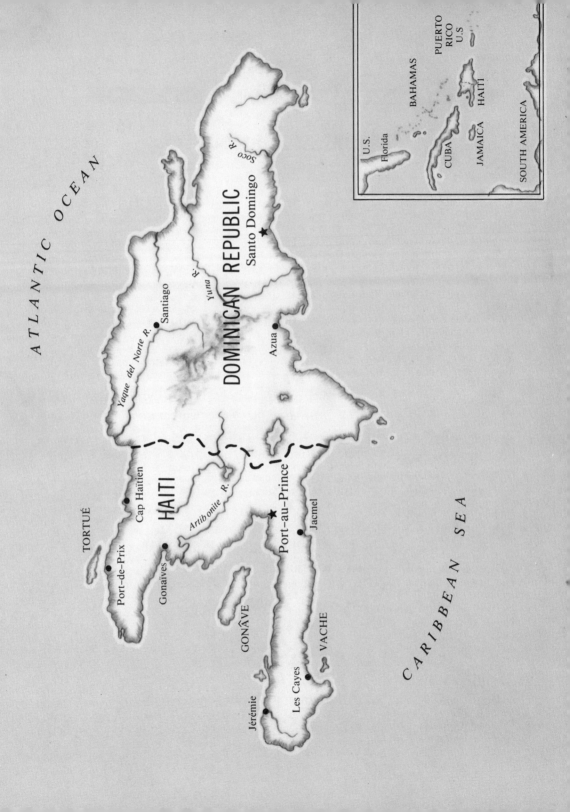

ATLANTIC OCEAN

CARIBBEAN SEA

DOMINICAN REPUBLIC

Santo Domingo

Soco R.

Yuna R.

Azua

Yaque del Norte R.

Santiago

HAITI

Cap Haïtien

TORTUÉ

Port-de-Prix

Gonaïves

Artibonite R.

GONÂVE

Port-au-Prince

Jacmel

VACHE

Jérémie

Les Cayes

BAHAMAS

PUERTO RICO U.S

U.S. Florida

CUBA

HAITI

JAMAICA

SOUTH AMERICA

believed to be an old Arawak Indian word for "land of mountains." Over two-thirds of the nation is of rugged mountainous terrain. Much of the exposed rock on the mountainsides is limestone.

Haiti is roughly divided into thirds, according to its land forms. The highest peaks are in the south, where the mountains stretch as high as 9,000 feet (2,700 m). Here is located Saddle Mountain, Haiti's highest peak. In the central area of the country the highest peaks reach only 7,000 feet (2,100 m), and in the north the mountain area can be described as hilly rather than mountainous. The Cibao Mountains, running from the northeast to the southwest, serve as the backbone of the island.

Most of Haiti's people live between the mountain ranges on one of three flat plains. These plains run east to west. Only half the acreage is arable (able to be farmed) today because of the erosion that has taken place over the centuries. Impoverished peasants, looking for fuel, were forced to cut down the trees that would have prevented soil erosion.

The three plains are the center of Haiti's agriculture. The largest of them is the Central Plain, which runs through the middle of the nation. Another, very different kind of plain is the marshland, along the border of the Dominican Republic. This land, called the Étang Sumatre, covers 70 square miles (180 sq km). The plains are crisscrossed by over one hundred small rivers and streams that help Haitian farmers irrigate their fields. The single longest river in Haiti is the Artibonite, which also extends into the Dominican Republic.

Haiti has lakes as well as rivers, but many of them contain salt water. Lake Azuey, a saltwater lake that is also shared with the Dominican Republic, has extremely blue-looking water because of its limestone bottom.

Haiti is an impoverished land.
Most of the people live in small
rural villages like this one on
the island of Tortue.

The Climate

Haiti's geography determines the climate of the nation. A tropical island, Haiti has the hot temperatures and rainy season characteristic of most tropical nations. Because of the mountains, however, rains do not always fall on the plains, where they are needed. The land in the lee (the side sheltered from the winds) of the mountains lacks rainfall. The climate is best in those parts of the island that are 2,000 feet (610 m) or more above sea level. Along the coast the climate is too hot to be pleasant for most people.

The temperature in the coastal areas ranges from 70° to 90° F (20° to 32° C) most of the time. Spring and early autumn are rainy seasons, when hurricanes are common. In addition to hurricanes, Haitians also have to worry about earthquakes. Major earthquakes have periodically wrought havoc on the country's economy and have also greatly affected political events. In 1966, Hurricane Cleo destroyed many Haitian farms. An earthquake in 1842 led to a revolution. A devastating hurricane in 1981 ruined much of the Haitian coffee crop.

As an island nation Haiti has many fishermen who are dependent on the island's ports and winds. In the days of sailing ships the Caribbean was easy to enter from the east, but it was difficult to leave because ships wishing to head east had to fight the northeast trade winds. Haiti itself is blessed by offshore winds that aid fishermen going out to sea in the morning and by onshore winds that blow them home at night. The northwestern ports face Cuba across the Windward Passage. The southwestern ports face Jamaica.

Plants and Animal Life

The climate of Haiti sustains a variety of tropical plant and animal life. High in the mountains, where the climate is more

moderate, the plant and animal life looks much like that of North America. Along the coast and lower slopes of the mountains grow yucca, mimosa, mahogany, logweed, and palm trees. At higher elevations oaks, pines, and other trees familiar to North Americans grow in abundance. Houses in Port-au-Prince and other Haitian cities have gardens full of bougainvillaea, gladiolus, oleander, and mimosa.

Citrus fruits grow throughout Haiti. Grapefruits, oranges, and limes are common. So are breadfruit, bananas, beans, cassava, rice, and sorghum. For three hundred years coffee and sugar have been the most highly cultivated crops.

The climate of Haiti that supports this variety of plant life also supports tropical animal life. Peacocks are common. Quits, hummingbirds, and flamingos flourish. Wild pigs run throughout the countryside. But the iguana, once a usual sight, is almost extinct today.

The People

Haiti has been called the "Daughter of Africa" because many of her 6 million people are descendants of African slaves. Perhaps as many as 95 percent of all Haitians have some African blood; it is the only nation in Latin America with such a high percentage of black people in its population. Most black Haitians are descendants of slaves who came from West Africa. During the

A cargo sloop sails into Port-au-Prince loaded with livestock, charcoal, and sisal fiber for sale.

later years of the slave trade, Africans from areas of central Africa were imported to Haiti as well.

Because of its predominantly black population, Haiti's history has been marked by racism. The Dominican Republic, a nation with a population that is 25 percent white and 75 percent mulatto, has long looked down on its blacker, poorer neighbor. Racist attitudes throughout the nineteenth century isolated Haiti from most other Latin American nations. And only in Haiti did black ex-slaves assume leadership positions immediately after independence.

In Haiti itself, however, racism has been a constant factor as well. Political prominence and social position have rested on the shade of a person's skin; mulattos (light-skinned descendants of black and white ancestors) frequently hold the most important posts. Not until the so-called Black Revolution of 1946 did Haitians firmly establish the complete equality—if not superiority—of black Haitians. François Duvalier, the black Haitian known as "Papa Doc," styled himself "Leader of the Blacks."

Although Haiti's leadership is predominantly black today, her peasant population is 100 percent black. Haitians share more customs with Africans than they share with other Latin Americans. As late as the 1950s Haitian mothers pierced and molded the heads and nostrils of their babies to shape their features, a custom handed down from their African ancestors. Parents also scarred their children's faces with hot cashew nuts as protection against the werewolf, who might carry away babies who were too beautiful. Infant mortality is so high in Haiti (at 20 percent, it is the highest in Latin America and among the highest in the world) that a child who lives to be two years old is called a *youn ti chape*—Creole for "escapee from death."

Seventy percent of all Haitians live in rural areas; Haiti has few cities. The largest is the capital city of Port-au-Prince, home

*Not far from the French-style
villas of the rich in Port-au-Prince,
the poor live in slums.*

to thousands of Haitian peasants and to the majority of the country's tiny wealthy élite. Strikingly beautiful French-style villas exist in the city, which is most notable for its foul slums. Cap Haïtien is Haiti's largest northern city and the oldest city in the country. The only other cities of any size are Les Cayes, Gonaïves, and Jérémie.

The Economy

Haiti had had an unfavorable balance of trade throughout most of its existence as an independent nation. This means that Haiti must buy more than it sells each year and that it is always in debt. Haiti sells coffee, sugar, lobsters, and bauxite. Its chief trading partner is the United States. Haitians must buy machinery, oils, textiles, flour, fish, vegetables, cars, paper, and most manufactured goods.

Most of Haiti's people are farmers. Agriculture in Haiti, however, has become poorer and poorer with each succeeding generation. The soil has badly eroded, and Haiti's farmers are too poor to be able to afford the fertilizers that would enrich the worn-out lands. With nearly three thousand people per square mile (2.59 sq km) of arable land, Haiti is the most overpopulated nation in the Western hemisphere. The shortage of land means that Haitian farmers cannot afford to rotate fields so that the land can rest and regain its productivity. They must force the land to produce whatever it can, even though this means less production and more poverty each year.

Coffee and sugar are the two main agricultural products. Each crop accounts for about 10 percent of Haitian exports every year. Haitian coffees are among the richest in the world. A poor coffee or sugar crop devastates the economy.

Although agriculture is the heart of the Haitian economy, the potential for industrial growth does exist. Bauxite is the only natural resource that has been fully tapped. In fact, much of Haiti's bauxite supply has been depleted. However, geologists have found deposits of iron ore, coal, manganese, silver, and other metals that have never been developed. Foreign companies, though, have been afraid to invest too much money in Haiti because of the unstable political situation. The United States has been the leading investor; in the past decade over two hundred American companies have created sixty thousand industrial jobs. This is very few in a nation of 6 million, over half of whom are unemployed. Furthermore, these companies exploit the need for work and do little to contribute to the development of the Haitian economy. In general they use unskilled Haitian labor at a minimum wage of thirty-three cents an hour. These Haitians help produce cheap products for re-export to the United States.

The average income for all Haitians, both farmers and industrial workers, is less than three dollars a day. Wealth is very uneven. One percent of the population earns 45 percent of the income. In the mid-1980s each person in Haiti accounted for less than three hundred dollars in output, compared with over thirteen thousand dollars per person in the United States, the wealthiest nation in the Western Hemisphere.

Since World War II, tourism has accounted for millions of dollars annually in the Haitian economy. In the early 1980s U.S. medical officials announced that Haitians were an especially high-risk group for the deadly disease AIDS (Acquired Immune Deficiency Syndrome). This announcement has scared away the Europeans and Americans who habitually visit Haiti's beaches and resort hotels, causing a loss of nearly $80 million annually.

Coffee and sugar cane are Haiti's main agricultural products. Here workers sort coffee beans. Facing page: Sugarcane plantation workers in a rural region of Haiti.

The Government

According to Haiti's constitution, written in 1964, the country is a democracy. It claims that "Haiti is an indivisible sovereign, independent, democratic and social republic." Under the Duvaliers, Haiti was a brutal dictatorship, not a democracy; but the constitution provided a structure for daily political life. Haiti is divided into nine districts. Each district is divided into communes. Communes are divided into wards if they are located in cities and into rural sections if they are located in the countryside.

The 1964 constitution also provided for a one-house (unicameral) legislature, with fifty-eight deputies elected every six years. This national legislature has the power to make treaties, to impeach the president, and by a two-thirds majority vote, to overrule presidential policies.

In spite of the power granted it by the constitution, the legislature under the Duvaliers rarely exercised leadership. Instead, it served as a "rubber stamp" for the dictatorship, saying yes to whatever the Duvaliers wanted.

By far the most influential government officials were the ministers who formed the cabinet of advisers surrounding the President. Men holding such positions as minister of labor and social work, minister of internal and national defense, and minister of foreign affairs and religions helped make the most important decisions. Nevertheless, the Haitian constitution provides a structure for a democratic government.

CHAPTER TWO

HAITI'S
SPECIAL CULTURE

In spite of the poverty of Haiti, the people have a rich culture and rich traditions that they have inherited from their many ancestors. These traditions have colored the Haitian language, religion, and arts.

Language

The official language of Haiti is French. However, very few Haitians learn French because schooling in Haiti is infrequent. French is spoken by government officials and their wealthy friends—the élite of Haiti. The French that these people speak is very stiff and formal; it is not the language of the people and does not change as new vocabulary comes into use.

The language that is spoken by most Haitians is called Creole. Creole is a unique blend of the many languages that different peoples have brought to the island over the past four hundred years. It is a combination of dialects from West and Central

Africa, sixteenth-century Spanish and Portuguese phrases, formal French, and the French of colonial sailors from Normandy and Brittany.

Creole was only a spoken language until the twentieth century. Then in 1948, Haitian scholars sponsored by the United Nations organization UNESCO began to write Creole and to develop spelling and grammatical rules for this language. Creole words are often spelled phonetically—as they sound in French—and not as they are spelled formally in modern French. For example, Haitians refer to God as Grand Met, meaning "Great Master." In French, *master* is spelled *maître*, but it is pronounced as if it were spelled *met*. Many Creole phrases are shortened, phonetic versions of words that represent what slaves heard their masters say. Because the slaves needed to communicate with their masters, they learned to mimic the sounds of the French words. Without education they did not include letters that were not pronounced. In return, the masters began to understand a handful of African—or Portuguese or Spanish or Breton—words that the slaves used. The mixed language that resulted formed the basis for modern Haitian Creole. Because so many Haitians use it, Creole is their real national language, even if French is the "official" national language.

Education

The UNESCO project that made Creole a written as well as a spoken language adopted a Creole slogan for its motto, *Ã non aprãn li ak écri*. This means, "Let us learn to read and write."

But fewer people know how to read and write in Haiti than in any other country in the Western Hemisphere. This has been true in Haiti for centuries. When Haiti was declared an independent nation in 1804, only 5 percent of its people knew how

This school in rural Haiti is typical
of an education system that
lacks adequate funding.
Fewer than 20 percent of Haitians
know how to read and write.

to read and write. Today, fewer than 20 percent of the people know how to read and write.

The 1964 Haitian constitution guaranteed free public education for all and made it mandatory that children attend elementary school. In spite of this, however, most Haitians do not attend school and never learn to read and write. First of all, there are too few schools and the country is too poor to build more. Secondly, there are very few schoolteachers.

Ten years after the 1964 constitution made elementary schooling compulsory, there were still only one and a half elementary school teachers for every fifty children in the country. In rural areas the situation was even worse. Fewer than 40 percent of the teachers worked in the rural areas where 70 percent of the people live. High school education was even rarer. There are fewer than one hundred high schools in all Haiti. Twenty-five percent of these are private high schools that educate the children of the élite.

Haiti has one national university, located in Port-au-Prince. In a recent class 40 percent of the students were studying for law degrees. Haiti has many needs—for doctors, engineers, social workers, and teachers. For the few young men and women of the Haitian élite who attend college, however, law is the most attractive career. It promises power and wealth in the circles of government.

Too few of Haiti's educated people have used their education to help others learn. The few educated people who have tried have often been critical of the government and its poor handling of education. As a result they have frequently been imprisoned or exiled from Haiti.

On any list of the failures of the Duvalier government, its failure to provide education for the majority of the people must rank near the top. One of the major goals of any new government in Haiti must be to educate the next generation of Haitians. Without education Haiti will never break away from its cycle of poverty.

Religion

Just as Haiti has two languages—an official one and one used by nearly everybody—the nation also has two religions. The official religion—that is, the one supported by the government—is Roman Catholicism. This is the religion that the French plantation owners brought to the island in colonial times. Just as the slaves learned basic French to communicate with their masters, so they also learned the basic beliefs of Roman Catholicism. Many were instructed in the religion by missionary priests who worked among the slaves. But side by side with their new Catholic faith the slaves retained parts of their African faith—the body of beliefs today known as voodoo.

The Fon people of West Africa—an area from which many of the colonial Haitian slaves were captured—have a word for spirit—*voudon*. In Creole *voudon* becomes *voudu* or *voodoo*. Voodoo is a religion, a philosophy, and a medical practice. It is also an attitude toward life that rests on total faith in the spiritual or divine world. Because of this absolute faith and because voodoo is a monotheistic (one god) religion, Haitians are content to belong to the Roman Catholic Church and to practice voodoo at the same time. Most believe that the voodoo spirits are similar to Catholic spirits and are available to deal with the everyday problems of life that God, the Grand Met, is too busy to worry about.

When the African slaves were transplanted to Haiti, they found that many of their daily needs were the same—health, water, children, food, music, and dancing. The spirits of the *voudon* of West Africa could serve them well in the new land, especially when they were lonely, scared, and brutally treated. Dancing and singing have long been part of voodoo ceremonies. Besides celebrating the religion, these joyous activities have provided generations of Haitians with relief from the misery of their daily life.

The voodoo religion is as highly structured as Roman Catholicism. Each voodoo spirit has been sent by God and is called a *loa*. Loas represent the good and bad forces in nature. For example, Ezili Freda is the loa of love, Zaka Mede is the loa of agriculture, Hegba is the loa of roads, and Baron Samedi is the loa of the cemetery or death. Shango is the loa of thunder and fire, and Damballah is the snake loa. People who believe in voodoo have a responsibility to serve the spirits to keep their daily lives running smoothly. Loas may enter people—possess them. From the behavior of the person who is possessed, people are able to identify which loa has entered the body.

Voodoo priests are called *houngans* or *oungans*. The chief priests are male. However, female priestesses, called *mambos*, are also very powerful. Lesser priests assist the *oungans* and *mambos* and may become priests themselves. The youngest assistants, male or female, are called *hounsi basale*. They may become *hounsi kanzo*, and then, after an ordeal by fire (in which they must dip their hands into pots of boiling oil), they may become the special servants of the *houngan* or *houngénicon*. The last stage, as apprentice *oungan*, is called *la place* for men

Participants in a voodoo religious ceremony appeal to the loa Kita to heal a sick child.

and *mambo* for women. Women may rise no higher than this. An *oungan*, when possessed by a loa, may perform amazing physical feats—for example, walk on coals or eat glass.

Haitian holidays are most often also the Roman Catholic religious holidays. The pre-Lenten season is the most joyous time of all. Saints' days are frequently combined with voodoo celebrations. For example, one important voodoo ceremony occurs each year on July 16, when faithful voodooists make a pilgrimage to Ville Bonheur. The walk is ordered by the loas, but the purpose of the pilgrimage is to worship the Roman Catholic Virgin of Miracles (*Vyej Mirak* in Creole) whose ghost allegedly appeared near there on top of a palm tree. Another celebration in July combines worship of the Ougu Feray, a loa of war, and Saint Jacques. A Saturday of dancing to voodoo drums is most often followed by Sunday-morning attendance at Roman Catholic mass.

Voodoo is also very important in providing medical treatment. *Oungans* are not witch doctors. They do practice healing, but their methods often include highly regarded herbal medicine. Haiti has fewer than one doctor for every five thousand people, so the *oungans* and *mambos*, with their practical medical help— particularly for everyday complaints—are necessary members of society.

Outsiders tend to focus on more exotic voodoo practices such as *pase poul*, in which an *oungan* brushes a live chicken over a sick person and then twists the head off the bird. Although animal sacrifice is part of voodoo, the daily medical practice of *oungans* and *mambos* is more likely to involve midwifery or herbal treatment for common illnesses. When a person has a sickness that cannot be treated, an *oungan* is there to explain the illness in terms of faith. Voodooists believe that diseases may be sent by spirits of ancestors when their descendants are not paying enough attention to them. Sick people may have angered the loas who were personally protecting them. Physical deformities are seen as messages from angry spirits, and the retarded are viewed as the unwilling carriers of the spirits of dead children.

The Arts

Voodoo has given Haitians their most distinctive music. The drum patterns that accompany voodoo celebrations and dancing are among the most sophisticated rhythms in the world. They are difficult to imitate and have yet to capture a widespread audience, but they are highly admired by musicians everywhere.

There is a saying that "every Haitian is an artist." Because there are so many Haitian paintings, their art was not taken seriously by most non-Haitian artists until very recently. About thirty years ago Haitian painting was "discovered." Primitive Haitian drawings, with their bright colors and realistic portraits of daily Haitian life, began to be highly valued by the international art world. A museum dedicated to Haitian painting was established in Port-au-Prince, Le Musée d'Art Haitien du College St. Pierre. Among the first Haitian artists to be famous outside of Haiti were André Pierre, Georges Liantaud, and Philomé Obin.

Much of Haitian literature in recent years has been political. Most writers have opposed Haiti's dictatorships and have sought through stories to reveal their evil. One of Haiti's most well-known novels is *Gouverneurs de la Rosée*, written in 1947 by Jacques Roumain. Another novel of the 1940s, *Canapé-Vert* by Philippe and Pierre Thoby-Marcelin, won the American Literary Prize in 1944.

Daily Life in Haiti

At least 4 million of Haiti's 6 million people live a peasant existence. Their homes are small huts with dirt floors and roofs made of thatched material or corrugated iron. There is little indoor plumbing or running water in the huts, yet Haitians pride themselves on their cleanliness.

Haitian money comes in two denominations, the *gourde* and the *centime*. A gourde is worth roughly twenty cents in U.S. money. A centime equals one one-hundredth of a gourde. That Haitians use such small amounts of money in their daily lives is another indication of what a poor country this is. With money so scarce, Haitians must help one another since they cannot afford to hire work to be done. A *coumbite* is a Haitian work party—friends and neighbors coming together to help with harvesting, planting, or building a hut. The work is accompanied by drums, and when the job is finished, the workers celebrate with drinks of *clairin*, a native rum.

Poverty affects all aspects of Haitian life, including weddings. A *plaçage* is an unofficial wedding that takes place without a priest. To have a proper church wedding requires shoes; many Haitians are too poor to own shoes, and so they are married in a nonchurch, unofficial ceremony. There may be as many as one hundred *plaçages* for every church wedding.

The Haitian diet is also affected by the poverty of the country. Because of high unemployment, anyone in a Haitian household who has a job gets to eat more than the other members of the family. Most work is difficult manual labor, and breadwinners need food for fuel to be able to do this hard work. The food the Haitians eat is divided into two categories—light and heavy. Heavy foods include cornmeal, boiled plantains, and potatoes; they are eaten early in the day in preparation for work. Light

*Haitian peasant women on
their way to market*

foods—soup, chocolate, and bread—are eaten at the end of the day.

Women in Haiti have carefully structured, traditional roles. Since 1950 they have had the right to vote. Before that a woman's public role was at the market. Haitian women walk long distances to market, usually carrying their goods in baskets balanced on their heads. Throughout much of Haiti's history men were frightened to go into public places such as the market for fear of being forced against their will into the armed forces. Marketing, an important part of daily life, was left to women.

Not all of Haiti's people are poor, but so many of them are that theirs is the way of life most characteristic of Haiti. The few very rich people lead lives like those of the very rich in other nations. They have large modern villas, expensive automobiles, many servants, and all the conveniences of modern life. In between is a tiny middle class, composed of shopkeepers, army officers, and petty bureaucrats. They will never enter the élite, and they must struggle not to return to the peasant class from which many of them have come. Most of the people in this small middle class live in cities.

CHAPTER THREE

INDIANS AND EUROPEANS IN HAITI

Some historians have said that Haiti's history began in 1492, when Columbus came to the island. That was indeed the beginning of its written history, but many people had been living in Haiti for hundreds of years before Columbus's arrival.

The Arawak

When the first Europeans landed on Hispaniola in the late 1400s, they found that the island was inhabited by Arawak Indians. The Arawak Indians numbered as many as one million at the time of the European "discovery." They had a highly sophisticated way of life. They lived in round huts in villages that contained as many as a thousand homes. They were farmers and raised such crops as manioc, maize, sweet potatoes, beans, peppers, arrowroot, papaya, peanuts, and avocados. They used fertilizers and irrigation methods to help grow their crops, and they traded among themselves and with Indians on other islands. They used both gold and silver for money. Besides their agricultural products, the Arawak also produced pottery, blankets, and polished stones for trade.

The Arawak had a well-developed political system. The people were ruled by chieftains. Among the Arawaks were trained warriors who used bows and poisoned arrows very effectively. Because Haiti was an island, many Arawaks were skilled sailors; they navigated the difficult winds of the Caribbean in canoes that held up to fifty passengers.

The end of the Arawak civilization came swiftly after the first landing of Europeans on Hispaniola. New diseases brought from Europe, such as measles and smallpox, plus massacres at the hands of European soldiers destroyed all the Arawak Indians less than fifty years after the first European landing. The most significant reminder of Arawak life in modern Haiti is the country's name; *Haiti* is an Arawak word.

Christopher Columbus and Spanish Exploration

Some historians neglect the Arawaks altogether; they believe that the history of Haiti began in 1492, when Christopher Columbus landed on the island in the course of his search for a passage to India. On December 25, 1492—Christmas Day—the

This drawing of the first Europeans to land on Hispaniola is believed to have been adapted from a sketch made at the time by Columbus.

Santa Maria, one of the three ships in Columbus's original fleet, ran aground on a reef near present-day Cap Haïtien. There Columbus established the first European settlement in the Western Hemisphere. Because it was Christmas Day when he landed, he named his village La Navidad, Spanish for "birthday of Christ," or Christmas. Columbus called the whole island—including modern Haiti and the Dominican Republic—La Isla Española, "the Spanish island." Hispaniola, a shortened version of this phrase, has remained the island's name.

Columbus left thirty-nine sailors from the *Santa Maria* at La Navidad to begin the work of settlement. He continued his exploration of the Caribbean and then returned to Spain. He claimed all the lands that he explored for Spain.

The Spanish king and queen, Ferdinand and Isabella, gave Columbus money for new ships to return to the Caribbean. When he returned to La Navidad about a year after leaving the *Santa Maria*'s sailors there, he found that all the Europeans were dead. They had been murdered by the Arawaks. In return, the Spanish massacred many of the Indians.

In spite of troubles with the Indians, La Isla Española became a major focus for Spanish colonization for the next twenty years. Spanish leaders such as Ponce de Léon, Juan de Esquivel, Nicolás de Ovando, and Diego Velásquez established villages throughout the island. Of the fifteen villages they established, five were located in present-day Haiti. Many of the settlements founded during this time were the beginnings of present-day Haitian cities. Puerta Real is modern Cap Haïtien; Verapaz is today a northern suburb of Port-au-Prince; Villanuevo de Yaquino is Jacmel; and Salvatierra de la Sabana is now known as Les Cayes. Wherever they met Indian resistance, the Spanish murdered the leaders and sold the other adults as slaves to Spanish farmers.

The French and the
Spanish on Hispaniola

The Spanish settlers were able to subdue the Indians very easily. However, they also faced a powerful European enemy who was far more difficult to subdue. This was France. The French, like the Spanish, wished to own an empire that would include the islands of the Caribbean.

French pirates had established strongholds on many islands throughout the Caribbean, including the island of Tortué. From there buccaneers—so called because of their practice of eating dried beef, or *boucan*—made raids on the Spanish settlements. Although the French pirates helped the French by attacking the Spanish settlements, they were still outlaws; the prizes and loot that they took from the Spanish did not help the French government because the pirates refused to pay taxes. The buccaneers were just as eager to kill Frenchmen who got in their way as they were to kill Spaniards. By the end of the 1600s the French military leaders in the Caribbean had gotten rid of pirates of all nationalities.

In 1639 a group of French exiles—members of a Protestant group known as Huguenots—settled on Tortué. A Spanish attack on Tortué in 1654 led these French people to flee to the northwestern mainland of La Isla Española, where they established a few permanent settlements around Cap Haïtien. The French referred to their western settlements as Saint-Domingue, while the Spanish called their eastern settlements Santo Domingo. The French established a provincial governor to rule their settlements. The first governor, appointed in 1665, was Bertrand d'Ogeron.

Louis XIV included Saint-Domingue in a list of his possessions in *des Indies*, as the French called the Caribbean islands.

In 1685 Louis's minister Colbert wrote a *Code Noir*, a set of rules for slavery in the West Indies. Around Cap Français the French were already building large plantations based on slave labor. Anticipating the time when all Saint-Domingue would belong to France, the French government began to establish rules for the society.

Throughout the 1500s the Spanish were the supreme European conquerors in the Caribbean. Although their greatest settlements were on the eastern half of La Isla Española, they also controlled the western half of the island. This situation changed in the seventeenth century. After a major defeat by the English in 1588, the Spanish lost much of their power in European politics. They entered the century of the 1600s much poorer than they had been in the 1500s. Because they were not as wealthy, they could not afford to pay as many sailors and soldiers as were necessary to protect their Caribbean possessions from other nations, especially France and England.

The French grabbed this opportunity to build up their strength on La Isla Española. Between 1600 and 1690 the French had established many successful settlements on Saint-Domingue, only to be driven out by the Spanish. Now it was their time to get even. Because Saint-Domingue had fewer Spanish settlements, they struck there first.

In 1690 a new French colonial leader emerged. This was Jean-Paul Tarin de Cussy. In 1684 the French government named de Cussy governor of Saint-Domingue, even though Saint-Domingue still officially belonged to the Spanish. In 1690 de Cussy led a French expedition against a major Spanish port, Santiago de los Caballeros. In 1691 the Spanish fought back by invading a French-held section of Saint-Domingue. De Cussy was killed, and the French were defeated at the battle of the Plain of Limonade. The Spanish attacked and burned Cap

Français, a major French settlement in the north of Saint-Domingue.

After de Cussy was killed, France appointed Jean-Baptiste du Casse to succeed him as governor. Du Casse faced a difficult task. The British had joined with the Spanish to try to eliminate the French from the Caribbean. During the middle 1690s the British attempted unsuccessfully to take several French possessions, including Saint-Domingue. Du Casse retaliated by attacking the island of Jamaica, a major English possession. Like the British, he was unsuccessful.

In 1696 du Casse began to rebuild the French sections of Saint-Domingue. He brought in more French settlers from St. Croix and successfully attacked several Spanish settlements. In 1697 the Spanish surrendered the western third of La Isla Española to the French. According to the Peace of Ryswyck, Saint-Domingue would be a French possession from then on; Haiti had passed into French hands.

Although the French owned Haiti for little more than a hundred years, their ownership made a far greater impression than Spanish ownership had made.

The French Plantations

The French wanted Saint-Domingue because they believed that the island's rich soil would be able to sustain profitable sugar plantations. They were right. Not only did they establish incredibly wealthy sugar plantations, they also found that Saint-Domingue could produce coffee, tobacco, cotton, and indigo crops. Under French control Saint-Domingue became the wealthiest European colony in the Western Hemisphere. By 1791, near the end of the period of French control, Saint-Domingue was exporting as much sugar as all the British West Indies combined.

By that time Saint-Domingue was clearly the most important French possession; her exports accounted for one-third of all French foreign trade. Saint-Domingue produced two-fifths of the world's sugar and one-half of the world's coffee.

The wealth of Saint-Domingue rested on the great plantations, especially the sugar plantations. The plantations in turn rested on black slave labor. The brutal slavery system is the key to understanding the tragedy and poverty of modern-day Haiti.

The first African slaves were brought to Haiti in 1510. By the time of the signing of the Peace of Ryswyck in 1697, there were eighteen thousand white French people and twenty-seven thousand black slaves in the French West Indies. The vast majority of these slaves lived on Martinique; only seven thousand lived in Saint-Domingue. By 1701, there was still the same number of whites living in the French West Indies, but the number of African slaves had nearly doubled. There were now forty-four thousand slaves, and the majority of them lived on the plantations of Saint-Domingue. Less than a century later, at the height of French Saint-Domingue's wealth, according to the census of 1788, there were twenty-eight thousand white people living in Saint-Domingue and over four hundred thousand slaves.

Slavery was a terrible system. Africans were brought to the West Indies against their will and forced to work for the plantation owners. Even on plantations where the slaveowners were relatively kind, certain facts were inescapable: Black people worked for white people for free. If they wanted to leave, they could not.

Slaves working on an eighteenth-century French sugar plantation

fig. 2.

Sugar was the most popular crop to grow because of the money it brought in trade and because sugar could be grown on the same land year after year. (Other crops, such as tobacco, wore out the land much more quickly.) Sugar growing was a very hard process that called for long hours of unskilled labor. *Crop*, the slaves' name for the spring of the year, when the cane was cut, pulled, and made into sugar, was the hardest time of the year. However, slaves were never idle at any time. During other times, known as *out of crop*, slaves planted new sugar cane. They were not trained to use even the simplest plows, so they were forced to dig the holes for the cane by hand.

For all their back-breaking work, slaves were provided with a thatch hut, two suits of clothing per year, a small weekly ration of food, and a tiny plot of land on which to grow yams, plantains, beans, and other products for their own use. If their family did not eat all that was grown, they were free to sell the extra at the market. A very few slaves were able to make enough money to buy their freedom; others were freed by their masters. By 1788 there were twenty-two thousand free blacks in Saint-Domingue. They were called *affranchis*, and they did not have the same political and social rights as the whites. They did have one great advantage over black slaves, however—they could keep whatever wages they earned.

By the end of the eighteenth century, when Saint-Domingue was at the peak of its prosperity, black slaves outnumbered the free people of the colony, white and black, by a ratio of 8 to 1. To control the thousands of slaves, Saint-Domingue had developed a rigid social system based on color. Any change in the system would upset the entire structure. Revolution—an idea that was spreading through North America and the mother country, France—proved to be the spark that set Saint-Domingue in flames.

CHAPTER FOUR

HAITI'S FIGHT FOR INDEPENDENCE

As the idea of revolution spread through North America, planters in Haiti began to think about rebelling against France. The idea of freedom meant different things to different people in Haiti. To the *affranchis* it meant equal rights with the white plantation owners. For the black slaves freedom meant an entirely new way of life.

Planter Society

The thousands of black slaves who were forced to work for the Saint-Domingue sugar planters had long wanted to be free. Every planter feared a slave revolt. Because there were so many more black people than white people in Saint-Domingue, the blacks were bound to win if they ever revolted. Slaves who tried to revolt against their masters were punished by death. Sometimes they were hanged, sometimes they were burned at the stake, and sometimes they were broken on the wheel.

Most of the time, however, the planters controlled the slaves by controlling the whole society. Saint-Domingue had a strictly ordered social structure. This means that people living there had very specific political rights and jobs. These were based on their skin color and family background.

At the very top of the social ladder were the French planters. By the 1780s, forty thousand white aristocrats were planters. The planters owned over two-thirds of all the arable land and two-thirds of all the slaves in the colony. The next most important group were the thirty thousand *gens de couleur*. These mulatto people were descended from white French planters, but they also had slave ancestors. The *gens de couleur* owned the other third of the land and slaves.

Next in line after these two property-owning groups were white people who did not own land or slaves. They were often shopkeepers, military personnel, or small bureaucrats. They were referred to as the *petits blancs* ("small whites") by the planters.

The *petits blancs* were followed by the freed slaves, or *affranchis*. Many of these were mulattos—children of slave mothers and planter fathers who were freed by their fathers. Others were slaves who had saved for years and years to buy their freedom. At the very bottom of this social ladder were the slaves. They greatly outnumbered all the others. Slave behavior was outlined in the 1685 Code Noir. An important provision of this code of laws provided that *affranchis* had the same rights as other free men, regardless of their color. In the eighteenth century the French government took this privilege away from the *affranchis*. Because of their color, they lost their political rights. In the coming revolution, this made them allies of the slaves.

The French Revolution

Saint-Domingue reached the height of its prosperity at exactly the same time when the French monarchy reached the height of its power. For many centuries French kings had lived in wealth and splendor in their palace at Versailles. By the 1780s the majority of the French people, who lacked food, clothing, and basic necessities, were tired of the luxurious wealth of the king. Louis XVI and his queen, Marie Antoinette, seemed very insensitive to the needs of their people. When told that the people of her country needed bread, the queen is reported to have said, "Let them eat cake." She had no idea that people who were starving for bread had no way to buy cake.

This unfeeling attitude on the part of the French king and queen led to their downfall. The French people revolted in 1789, killed the monarchs, and established a new republican form of government that promised freedom and equality for all French citizens.

The ideas of revolution and freedom crossed the ocean to the French colony. To the different members of Saint-Domingue society, the ideals of the French Revolution meant different things. The colonial planters wanted the freedom to rule the colony on their own, without having the mother country make their laws—especially tax laws. The mulatto planters believed that the revolution promised them an opportunity to get back the political rights they had once had; in 1766 the French minister of the marine had barred the *gens de couleur* from voting or holding political office.

For the slaves, of course, the Revolution promised freedom. The slavery situation in Saint-Domingue had worsened in recent years, and it continued to do so in the first few years of the French Revolution. Greedy for ever greater sugar profits, the planters had purchased greater numbers of slaves. In 1788 Saint-Domingue imported thirty thousand more slaves from Africa; nearly half of all slaves crossing the Atlantic that year were purchased by Saint-Domingue planters. Between 1789 and 1791 the slave population grew from 450,000 to 480,000. As more and more slaves were forced onto the island's plantations against their will, trouble was bound to occur. The French Revolution publicized the idea that all people should be free. Saint-Domingue's slaves were ready to believe this and to act on that belief.

The New French Republic
and Saint-Domingue

In 1791 the *gens de couleur* took the first step when they sent representatives to the French National Assembly to plead with the Assembly to grant them political rights. They found that the members of the Assembly, a revolutionary group of people, had no liking for the wealthy Saint-Domingue planters. The planters, living in great wealth while their slaves starved and suffered, seemed to the members of the Assembly to be just like Louis XVI and Marie Antoinette.

Within the National Assembly an especially radical group, the Société des Amis de Noirs (the Society of Friends of Black People), wanted the French planters on Saint-Domingue to free their slaves. The Marquis de Lafayette, a friend of George Washington and a hero of the American Revolution, was an important member of this group. As a first step in equalizing all people of the colony, the National Assembly issued a decree in May 1791 granting political privileges to all free people in the colony, regardless of race.

This decree greatly angered the white planters in the colony. The year before, they had murdered a free mulatto, Vincent Ogé, for attempting to rally the *gens de couleur* on the island. Ogé had become a martyr to the mulatto cause. The *gens de couleur*, however, were not anxious to have all the slaves freed. Many of them were slaveowners themselves. They simply wanted to share the power of the white planters.

This was not to be. Once the social structure had shifted even a little bit, it was impossible for the French planters to maintain control. Once the idea of freedom had entered the colony, it could not be stopped. Slaves as well as *gens de couleur* demanded their rights.

Revolution

In August 1791 the slaves in the northern part of Saint-Domingue revolted, massacring white planters and destroying crops, irrigation systems, barns, machinery, and houses. Great sugar plantations were destroyed and would never be rebuilt.

In the western part of the colony the white planters warred against the mulattos. The same thing happened in the south, where white planters went so far as to arm their slaves as protection against attacking bands of mulattos.

The white planters used the French Revolution cry of "Liberty" to declare their freedom from the mother country. They wanted the freedom to continue to repress the black slaves and free *gens de couleur*. Their plan backfired. Freedom and liberty spread through the colony, but the white ruling class lost its power forever.

Between 1792 and 1802 Saint-Domingue was plunged into terrible warfare. By the time it ended, a new nation had come into being, but the economy of the old nation had been so completely destroyed by the war that the new nation was destined to be impoverished.

Many groups were involved in the Saint-Domingue revolution. In 1792 six thousand French troops under the direction of

*French troops putting down a slave revolt
in eighteenth century Saint-Domingue*

Léger Félicité Sonthonax landed in the colony. Sonthonax was a radical Jacobin who believed that freedom meant freedom for all. He sided with the mulattos at first. Then in 1793 the National Assembly in Paris voted to abolish slavery in the French colonies. Sonthonax joined with the rebellious black troops in the north and helped them destroy the white planters.

Meanwhile, the French had European enemies who wanted to capture the colony as well. Both the British and the Spanish sent troops to try to capture Saint-Domingue for their countries. In March 1794 the British were successful in occupying Port-au-Prince. The Spanish, meanwhile, concentrated on Santo Domingo, their former colony on the eastern end of Hispaniola. Spanish troops based in Santo Domingo mounted attacks on Saint-Domingue.

Toussaint L'Ouverture

Out of the fighting a great leader emerged, a black man who would lead Saint-Domingue to independence. François Dominique Toussaint L'Ouverture had been born a slave in 1743. He had been taught to read and write by his master. (To repay his master for this kindness, Toussaint helped him escape to the United States during the revolution.)

Although Toussaint was a northern slave, he did not participate in the original slave rebellion in 1791. He did leave his plantation at that time to become the leader of a band of forty thousand black troops. Toussaint hired out his forces to the Spanish army at first. When the Spanish joined the English invaders in 1794, Toussaint feared that the Europeans wished to reestablish slavery. He then joined Sonthonax and the republican French army.

In 1795 the Spanish withdrew from the war in Saint-

Domingue. France and Spain signed the Treaty of Bâle, which gave Santo Domingo to France. By now, however, Napoleon Bonaparte had seized power in France. One of his brothers controlled Spain, so in spite of the treaty, Spanish troops were left in Santo Domingo.

By 1798, Toussaint was the leading French republican fighter. In that year he and his troops were successful in forcing the British to withdraw from Saint-Domingue. Now Toussaint had only one enemy left—a mulatto force in the south operating under the command of General André Rigaud. Rigaud wanted the mulattos to gain control over the blacks.

Toussaint defeated Rigaud in 1800. During the course of the fighting, ten thousand mulattos were massacred, the valuable irrigation works in the Artibonite River were destroyed, and Les Cayes, the third largest city in the colony, was devastated. Upon the surrender of the mulatto forces, Toussaint controlled the country.

Toussaint's Rule

The country he controlled was weary of war, badly scarred by over a decade of fighting, and totally destroyed economically. Repairing the disorder seemed to be an impossible task. However, Toussaint was a great leader, and he began his work immediately.

First, he appealed to the French government to name him governor-general of Saint-Domingue. He ordered an end to the mulatto massacres, established a commercial treaty with Eng-

Toussaint L'Ouverture (1743–1803),
the greatest leader in Haiti's history

land, and encouraged some white planters to return to the colony to help rebuild the colony's agriculture. In 1801 Toussaint's troops expelled the Spanish from Santo Domingo, and Toussaint freed the slaves in that part of the island.

In that same year, Toussaint wrote a new constitution for Saint-Domingue. In it he mentioned that Saint-Domingue was a French state, but he declared himself dictator for life with the right to name his own successor. The abolition of slavery was affirmed.

This new constitution infuriated Napoleon Bonaparte. He felt that Toussaint's title of dictator for life was an insult to his own dictatorship. Napoleon believed that the French Empire had room for only one dictator, and he wanted to get rid of the "gilded African," as he called Toussaint.

Furthermore, Napoleon had decided that the restoration of slavery in the colony would mean the restoration of the sugar plantations and their great revenues for the French government. In 1802 war broke out again. General Victor LeClerc, Napoleon's brother-in-law, landed at Cap Français in January. By June he had defeated Toussaint and had shipped him to France, where he later died in prison.

The imprisonment and death of Toussaint did not mean success for the French, however. The fighting went on under Jean-Jacques Dessalines, one of Toussaint's chief supporters. In November General LeClerc died of yellow fever. During 1802

The arrest of Toussaint L'Ouverture by the French General LeClerc in 1802. Toussaint was sent to France where he died in prison.

and 1803 forty thousand French troops died in Saint-Domingue, some from fighting and many, like General LeClerc, from disease. When war broke out in Europe in 1803, Napoleon could no longer afford to fight in Saint-Domingue.

On January 1, 1804, Jean-Jacques Dessalines declared Saint-Domingue independent of France. The French withdrew their troops. Henceforth Saint-Domingue would be the independent nation known as Haiti.

The price of liberty had been high. All the progress that Toussaint had made was destroyed during the fighting with LeClerc's troops. The leaders of the new nation had difficult times ahead of them.

CHAPTER FIVE

HAITI'S FIRST CENTURY OF FREEDOM

With the declaration of independence in 1804, Haiti became the second colony in the Western Hemisphere to gain freedom from the Old World; the United States had been the first. Sadly for Haiti, the first century of her independence was not as successful as that of the United States. There were many reasons for this. First, the fight for independence had destroyed the Haitian economy. Second, because the new Haitian leadership was black, other nations—especially the United States, where slavery still flourished—refused to help the new nation. Third, the Haitian rebels themselves did not hold true to the ideals of freedom and equality for which they had fought. They merely replaced the French dictatorship with a local dictatorship.

A Divided Haiti

When Jean-Jacques Dessalines declared Haiti's independence, he also announced that he was the first emperor of Haiti, Jacques I.

He became a harsh ruler. A former slave, he had been born in Africa. Dessalines had murdered his master, a free Negro, during his escape from slavery. He was extremely intolerant of the former plantation owners, and at one point he ordered his troops to kill all whites. Dessalines also tried to rid the country of voodoo—an unpopular action. His cruelty prevented him from being an effective ruler. Although he had been a loyal supporter of Toussaint, he was unable to carry on Toussaint's program of economic rebuilding. Jacques I's reign was brief. He was assassinated in 1806.

After Jacques I died, the new nation was badly divided. In the north the former black slaves, who had first begun the revolution in 1791, supported a former slave, Henri Christophe. The mulatto population that dominated the southern half of the nation supported a mulatto leader, Alexandre Pétion. For the next 150 years blacks and mulattos fought over the leadership of Haiti. Racism proved to be a divisive factor in Haitian politics.

In December 1806, after the death of Jacques I, Christophe and his followers called for a constitutional convention. Pétion and his followers opposed the constitution proposed by Christophe. The convention then wrote a compromise constitution that neither side liked very much. Haiti, according to this plan of government, would be a republic. There would be a powerful senate and a weak presidency. Although Christophe could have been president, he refused the office because he felt that the position was not powerful enough.

Christophe returned home to the north, called for a new convention, and in 1807 was elected president for life. A new form of dictatorship had come to Haiti. Meanwhile, in the south, Pétion's followers elected him president in 1808. Haiti was now divided in half, with two presidents.

Pétion was the son of an *affranchi*, a freed slave whose

father had been a white planter. Pétion had been educated in France; like most mulattos he felt himself superior to the masses of illiterate black Haitians. He planned to rebuild the economy of southern Haiti by subdividing the land into small peasant plots, on which each family could grow food to support themselves.

In the north, Christophe attempted to rebuild the great estates. Coffee replaced sugar as the major cash crop. In 1791, when the revolution began, Saint-Domingue had exported over 160 million pounds (73 m kg) of sugar. In 1820 sugar exports totaled slightly over 2,000 pounds (907 kg). On the other hand, coffee exports in 1791 had totaled 68 million pounds (30.6 m kg). By 1825, Haiti was exporting nearly 40 million pounds (18 m kg) of coffee.

In 1816, Pétion's followers named him president for life. He had given land to soldiers and peasants—a practice that followed the ideals of the revolution. However, he, too, had become a dictator. Although he controlled his own country, Pétion supported other Latin American nations in their struggles for freedom. In 1814 and 1815 he allowed Simón Bolívar, the great South American freedom fighter, to hide out in Haiti.

Pétion understood the value of education. In 1816 he opened the first high school in Port-au-Prince. By the time of Pétion's death in 1818, the southern half of Haiti was certainly the richer section of the country.

Henri I

In spite of Pétion's contributions to Haiti, Henri Christophe is the better known of the two rulers. In 1811 he declared himself King Henri I. He changed the name of Cap Haïtien to Cap Henri and wrote a new code of laws, the Code Henri. He also established schools, a theater, and a newspaper.

The people of northern Haiti, former black slaves, lived as serfs in Henri I's kingdom. The Code Henri set down rules for people's behavior. In addition to big rules about theft and murder, the Code Henri also had little rules. For example, people were prohibited from entering the capital unless they were wearing shoes.

The greatest monument to Henri I was the citadel, La Ferrière, that he ordered his people to build for him. This great fortress was designed to protect Haiti from invasion. It was built 8 miles (13 km) from the city of Milot on top of a mountain, Bonnet à L'Évêque.

The great fort was built of stone, with walls that were 100 feet (30 m) high and 20 feet (6 m) thick. Three hundred cannon were mounted on the walls. All the stones and cannon had to be carried by men up the mountainside. Henri forced people to do this work. Haitian legends say that for every one of the fort's twenty thousand stones, a man died because the work was so dangerous. Henri estimated exactly how long it should take a gang of men to haul a cannon to the fortress. If the group did not work fast enough, every tenth man was killed. This practice made the men work faster. According to another legend, Henri hired two French architects to design the fort. When the work was completed, he had the Frenchmen pushed off the walls to their deaths so that they could never reveal the secret entrances to the citadel.

Although La Ferrière has been badly damaged by earthquakes over the years, its ruins remain a tribute to the cruelty

La Ferrière, the citadel,
built during the reign of Henri
Christophe at great sacrifice of life

and determination of Henri I. Not only was it Henri's residence, it was also the place where he died. In April 1820, Henri was taken ill. He may have been poisoned. After six months of illness, Henri realized that he was losing his power because of his weakened condition. He shot himself in October 1820. According to Haitian legend, he killed himself with a silver bullet.

Jean-Pierre Boyer

After Alexandre Pétion died in 1818, he was succeeded by another mulatto, Jean-Pierre Boyer. Boyer assumed power in the south, but after the death of Henri I he reunited the two halves of the nation. Boyer remained president of Haiti from 1818 to 1843—the longest period of time that anyone has headed the country.

Boyer's followers, most of whom were educated mulattos, called themselves the élite. Many of them had lived in France, and they supported Boyer's plan to reestablish friendly relations with that nation. In 1825, Haiti and France signed a treaty in which France recognized Haiti's independence, in return for which Haiti agreed to pay France 150 million francs over five years in compensation for the destruction of French property during the revolution. This was a very large sum of money for the struggling, poverty-stricken new nation. However, Boyer believed that Haiti would be able to pay because he had recently added Santo Domingo to the nation.

In 1821 the Spanish people of Santo Domingo had followed Haiti's example and rebelled against their mother country, Spain. This pleased Boyer and the people of Haiti. For many years they had feared that the French would use Santo Domingo as a base from which to invade Haiti and regain possession of their colony.

In 1822, however, less than one year after the Santo Domingo rebellion, the Haitian army invaded and conquered Santo Domingo. Boyer announced that Santo Domingo would now be part of Haiti, called La Partie de l'Est. This was the second time Haiti controlled its neighbor. (After Toussaint freed the slaves in Santo Domingo in 1801, Haitians had fled to the country. Not until 1808 had the Spanish in Santo Domingo resumed control of their part of the island.)

For two decades after Boyer's invasion, Santo Domingo remained in Haitian hands. But this new part of Haiti resented Boyer's control. There were racial, language, and cultural differences between the Haitians and the Dominicans. The Code Henri was substituted for Spanish law, Spanish landholdings were confiscated, and the University of Santo Domingo was closed down.

Most upsetting to the Dominicans, however, was the Haitian insistence that the money that the Haitians had agreed to pay France now would be paid by all of Haiti, including La Partie de l'Est. Although Boyer managed to keep control over Santo Domingo, the Spanish there were ready to rebel at any opportunity. From 1838 on, a secret organization called La Trinitaria planned "for our permanent separation from Haitian rule and the establishment of a free and sovereign republic . . . that shall be called the Dominican Republic." The Dominicans wanted total freedom from Haiti and its debts.

In 1842 a natural disaster struck. A terrible earthquake shattered the northern half of Hispaniola and destroyed many villages and towns. Besides the loss of life, Haiti also suffered a loss of income. Boyer could not afford to pay his armies, and the soldiers stationed in Santo Domingo were willing to let the province rebel successfully against Haiti.

Boyer was too busy in the main part of Haiti to prevent the Dominicans from separating and forming their own government. In January 1843 a fire destroyed much of Port-au-Prince. Faced with natural disasters, a weakened economy, a rebellious army, and hungry citizens, Boyer abdicated in April 1843. The Haitians claimed they wanted a democracy.

Haiti in the Second Half
of the Nineteenth Century

For four years after Boyer's abdication, Haiti was ruled by a succession of weak presidents, none of whom could bring order to the country. Then in 1847, in an attempt to unify the nation, the élite supported the appointment of a black former slave, Faustin Soulouque. He was called Emperor Faustin I. Democracy in Haiti had ended once again.

Faustin I was overthrown in 1859, and a new attempt was made to make Haiti a republic. General Fabré Geffrard, a dark mulatto supported by the élite and by the majority of Haiti's black people, became president. Geffrard remained in office until 1867, when he lost control of the army and was overthrown. During his time in office he accomplished several things. First, he developed a good relationship with the Vatican. This was important because many of Haiti's people were Roman Catholic, and Catholicism was the official religion of the country.

During General Geffrard's rule the United States' Civil War took place. He took this opportunity to increase Haiti's cotton production, an important boost to the Haitian economy. Haiti, with its history of black slavery, strongly supported the northern states in the Civil War. In return Abraham Lincoln granted diplomatic recognition to Haiti in 1864. This was very important for the black nation.

From the time of General Geffrard's overthrow until the end of the nineteenth century, Haiti was ruled by a succession of presidents, most of whom were army officers. Although Haiti claimed to be a democratic country, each of these presidents was really a dictator. Often they used the army as a police force to make people do things their way.

There were two political parties in Haiti during this time. One, the Liberals, was supported by the mulattos, and the other, the Nationals, drew most of its support from the descendants of black slaves. Both parties, however, were controlled by members of the élite.

Two of the many presidents during this time lasted longer than the others. From 1879 to 1888, Haiti had a black president, Louis-Félicité Lysius Saloman. During his presidency Saloman established a national bank, ended the payments to France, and brought internal order.

Saloman was followed by Florvil Hyppolite, who served as president of Haiti from 1889 to 1896. Hyppolite helped modernize Haiti. He built railroads, telegraph and telephone systems, new roads, docks, and bridges to improve Haiti's transportation and communications.

During most of this time Haiti had excellent relations with the United States, the most powerful nation in the Western Hemisphere. In 1870, Haiti had even tried to give the United States the harbor at Môle St. Nicolas. This harbor, with its command of the Windward Passage, was one of Haiti's greatest resources. In return for the harbor Haiti wanted the Americans to pay Haiti's debt to France.

Not until the late 1880s did the United States see the value of Môle St. Nicolas. By then Haiti was no longer interested in giving up the harbor, and relations between the two nations were not as friendly. The United States would play a large and not always welcome role in Haiti during the twentieth century.

CHAPTER SIX

TWENTIETH-CENTURY HAITI

For a hundred years independent Haiti led a troubled existence. Political upheaval, natural disasters, and poor economic conditions combined to make Haiti a very unstable country. Then, in the early part of the twentieth century, the United States began a new foreign policy with regard to its southern neighbors in the Western Hemisphere. Nations like the Dominican Republic, Nicaragua, Cuba, and Haiti found that Americans were willing to step in and help improve conditions in their countries. However, the United States often did not wait to be invited. Furthermore, in return for the aid it gave, it expected to have a powerful voice in how the countries it helped ran their governments.

Haiti Enters the Twentieth Century

By the time the twentieth century opened, Haiti had made very little progress in the years since its independence. In fact, the greatest accomplishment of the tiny island nation in its first century of freedom was to manage to remain free. The country had resisted tempting offers from the United States to buy the strategic harbor at Môle St. Nicolas. (At one point the United States had even offered to buy all of Haiti in order to gain access to Môle St. Nicolas.)

Between the presidency of General Fabré Geffrard (1859–1867) and 1915, all but one president of Haiti was a military officer; only officers were able to capture the office. Elections were dishonest, and to become president a person had to use force. The army was the force that most of the officers used.

When things did not improve economically, the army would become dissatisfied and turn to a new leader. Since the presidents at the end of the nineteenth century and at the beginning of the twentieth century were not successful in changing the basic economic problems in Haiti, they lasted a very short time before being replaced. If they were lucky, they were simply thrown out of office. Many, however, were assassinated.

Between 1911 and 1915 seven presidents met violent ends. In August 1911, General Antoine Simon was overthrown by revolution. His successor, Cincinnatus LeConte, was blown up in an explosion at the palace. In August 1912, President Tancrede Auguste assumed the office, and nine months later he was poisoned. The president after him, Michael Oreste, managed to flee to Jamaica when his presidency ended after seven months. The next president, Orestes Zamor, was imprisoned and murdered after eight months. Then Davilmar Theodore held the presidency for three months before he was overthrown.

In July 1915 President Vilbrun Gillaume Sam ordered many prominent Haitians to be arrested and killed in an attempt to keep control of the government. When people rebelled, Sam tried to flee Haiti. He hid at the French embassy in Port-au-Prince.

His Haitian subjects were outraged. The country was bankrupt; soldiers were getting a three-foot stalk of sugar cane each week as their only food ration. A mob of angry Haitians dragged the president from the French embassy and brutally killed him.

U.S. Intervention

President Woodrow Wilson ordered U.S. Marines to enter Haiti and restore stability in the country. In other countries the United States ordered interventions to protect American investments, but this was not the case in Haiti. Because of Haiti's poverty, it was not important to the United States either as a market or as a place for investments. Haiti sold the bulk of its most profitable crop—coffee—not to the United States but to France.

In 1915 the total of all U.S. investments in Haiti was $4 million. Most of this money had been invested by two New York companies. In comparison, $4 million was only 1.8 percent of U.S. money invested in Cuba and .05 percent of that invested in Mexico.

The United States was interested in Haiti not because of investments but because of its fear that Germany might take advantage of Haiti's instability and use Haiti as a base from which to invade the United States. World War I began in Europe in 1914. The British, French, and Russians were battling the Germans and Austro-Hungarians. Although the United States did not enter the war until 1917, it was already clear that the United States, if it entered the war, would fight with England against Germany. The Americans wanted to make sure that Germany would be kept out of the Western Hemisphere.

Shortly after two thousand U.S. Marines landed in Haiti, a new presidential election was held. Philippe Sudre Dartiguenave was elected president. The new president negotiated a treaty with the United States. The United States agreed to help the Haitians recover from their bankruptcy by paying off the Haitian debt. That way Haiti would owe money only to the United States, and the Americans would not have to worry about other nations invading Haiti in order to get their money.

The U.S. Marines immediately embarked on a campaign to clean up Haiti's major problems. The United States developed plans for building new roads, installing sewer systems, and providing other public health facilities. There were plans for building schools, training teachers, and establishing a strong local police force to help the president keep law and order in Haiti.

Although most of these measures seemed positive, the Haitians themselves were not always happy about the way the president and the marines went about their work. In 1916 President Dartiguenave announced that he was restoring the corvée, a system of forced labor that dated back to slavery and that had not been used since the cruel days of Henri I. Under a corvée unemployed men were forced to work on government projects whether they wanted to or not. By using the corvée, Dartiguenave hoped to have cheap labor to complete the U.S. projects and also to help the country's unemployed people find work.

Because of the corvée and other repressive measures, there was an uprising of Haitians who did not like what the United States intervention was doing to Haiti. Led by Charlemagne Péralte, a black Haitian, as many as twenty thousand rural Haitians revolted against the government. It took the president, his police, and the U.S. Marines two years to subdue the uprising. Seven U.S. Marines, twenty-seven local police, and over two thousand Haitian rebels were killed. More Haitians lost their lives during these two years of fighting than during all the other uprisings since Haiti's independence.

The Péralte uprising slowed the many projects that had begun in 1916. By 1921, many of Haiti's debts were still unpaid, there had been no progress in public education, and only one road had been built, from Cap Haïtien to Port-au-Prince.

The rebellion pointed out one of the most negative aspects of U.S. occupation. The U.S. Marines and the U.S. ambassadors to Haiti had brought with them American racial prejudices. The people they supported in Haitian politics—like Dartiguenave—were light-skinned mulattos. For most Americans, the lighter-skinned the person, the more acceptable he or she was. The Haitians who were forced into the corvée and who then rebelled were black Haitians. Throughout the U.S. occupation, this ugly racism created tension.

Perhaps one of the most positive contributions the Americans made to Haiti was their help in writing a democratic constitution. In 1917, U.S. Assistant Secretary of the Navy Franklin D. Roosevelt drafted a constitution for Haiti. In this constitution, all Haitians were considered equal. The constitution was presented to the Haitian Congress, but they refused to approve it. The United States then called for a plebiscite—a vote by all the people—to be overseen by the U.S. Marines. The constitution was approved. Nearly one hundred thousand Haitians voted for the constitution of 1918; fewer than one thousand voted against it. The vote was so lopsided that most people then believed and most historians later believed that the election was unfair. They think that many people did not understand what they were voting for—not surprising in a country where so few people knew how to read and write. It is possible that the U.S. Marines told people how to vote.

There were two reasons the Haitian Congress did not want the constitution. First, under the constitution of 1918, foreigners were permitted to own property in Haiti. Haitians feared that

The U.S. Marines in Haiti in 1916.
Here they search for hidden arms.

rich foreigners would buy the best land and eventually take control of the country—a situation not unlike the days of the French planters. Secondly, the constitution made the police force the only legal armed force. Under Dartiguenave the police force had served as the private police for the president rather than as a law enforcement agency serving all the people of Haiti. Haitians did not want to see this happen again.

In 1922, Louis Borno, another president handpicked by the Americans, replaced Dartiguenave. Under Borno's rule a number of reforms took place. He negotiated a forty-million-dollar loan from the United States. Railroads were built, telephones and electricity were installed (at least in the cities), and water purification systems were installed. A few new hospitals were built, and vaccines were made available to portions of the population who had never had access to modern health practices.

In 1929, Haiti and other Caribbean nations were represented at a conference in Havana that was called to consider problems common to the region's countries. Haitian representatives explained that Haiti disliked having U.S. forces in Haiti. Partly because of this feeling but also because an economic depression in the United States made Americans unwilling to spend money in Haiti, U.S. President Franklin D. Roosevelt prepared in 1933 for the withdrawal of the U.S. Marines from Haiti. In 1934 they left.

Before Roosevelt withdrew the marines, he made sure that Haiti had a stable president who was friendly to the United States. In 1930, Sténio Vincent, a mulatto and leading Port-au-Prince lawyer, had been chosen president with U.S. approval. After the marines were withdrawn, Vincent had a loyal, well-trained local police force to help him rule Haiti. His presidency lasted until 1941.

Vincent's biggest problems came from Haiti's neighbor, the

Dominican Republic. Like Haiti, the Dominican Republic had been plagued by unstable governments, a shaky economy, and intervention by U.S. Marines. In 1930 a powerful dictator took over the Dominican Republic. His name was General Rafael Trujillo, the "strong man" of the Dominican Republic for over three decades.

Trujillo had no love for Haiti. When he took control of the Dominican Republic, there were many Haitians working in the western half of that nation. The Dominican Republic had fewer than two hundred people per square mile in comparison with Haiti's four hundred per square mile, so Haitians living near the border looked for work in the less-crowded Dominican Republic.

In 1937, Trujillo ordered a purge of all Haitians living in the Dominican Republic. Between ten thousand and twenty thousand Haitians were cruelly murdered by Trujillo's troops. Haiti was too poor to send an army to fight back. Haitian bitterness about the Dominicans lasted for a long time.

In 1941, Vincent left office. The president who succeeded him was another member of the mulatto élite, Elie Lescot. The University of Haiti was established during the presidency of Lescot, but his years in office were otherwise relatively undistinguished. In 1946 he was deposed by the police force.

The next president, Dumarsais Estimé, was the first black to hold the presidency since 1915. His election in 1946, known as the Black Revolution, marked the end of the dominance of the mulatto élite. Estimé's government wrote a new constitution that reflected the desires of the majority of black Haitians. He ended foreign property ownership in Haiti, supported labor rights, and instituted an income tax that forced the high-income élite to pay more taxes. During Estimé's rule, many diseases that had afflicted Haitian people were wiped out. Doctors sponsored by the government attacked yaws, malaria, typhoid, and tuberculosis.

Because the attack on these diseases was so successful, the population of Haiti grew more rapidly. This rapid growth in population meant more hunger and more poverty. The increased hunger and poverty led to a general dissatisfaction with Estimé and his government. In May 1950 a military triumvirate overthrew Estimé.

Soon one member of the triumvirate, Paul Magloire, became president of Haiti. Although the election was probably rigged, Magloire seemed to be a sensitive leader. He wanted to improve the health and education of Haitians and the productivity of the country. Magloire lost control of the army, however, and like many Haitian presidents he was thrown out of office by a military coup.

Fifteen years of political instability, a restless army, and a hungry, discontented population meant that Haiti was ripe for a strong-arm dictator like the one in the Dominican Republic. The man who took this opportunity and seized control of the country was as powerful and as cruel as General Trujillo. Dr. François Duvalier became president of Haiti.

CHAPTER SEVEN

THE DUVALIERS
AND AFTER

In 1957, Haiti needed a government that would continue to work for improved health conditions, a rebuilt economy, the modernization of roads, water facilities, and industry, and increased public education. Instead they got another dictator. During his presidency conditions in the country deteriorated rather than improved.

Papa Doc

Dr. François Duvalier, known to Haitians as "Papa Doc," rose to national prominence through his work in the campaigns to wipe out malaria and yaws. He was a black country doctor, but he had political ambitions. Papa Doc did not want to spend his life curing poor people of disease.

Papa Doc knew how powerful the influence of voodoo was on the Haitian people. He used their belief in voodoo to help keep himself in power. Haitians believe that Baron Samedi, the loa of the cemetery or death, dresses all in black. Papa Doc dressed like Baron Samedi. He always wore a black hat, a black suit, and dark sunglasses. Poor, illiterate Haitians sometimes confused Papa Doc with Baron Samedi. They appealed to Duvalier to send plagues to their enemies, the same way they would appeal to a loa. Many Haitians believed that Papa Doc could read the future, that he slept in a grave once a year, and that he kept the dried heads of his enemies in his office. Papa Doc also changed the colors of the Haitian flag from red and blue to red and black —the colors of secret societies. By seeming to have the power of voodoo supporting him, Papa Doc quickly won the support of the people.

In addition to voodoo, Papa Doc had another very effective way of controlling the people. He developed a powerful private police force, the Tonton Macoutes, who terrorized anyone who opposed Duvalier's policies. Again Papa Doc borrowed from voodoo. In Haitian mythology Tonton Macoute is the name of a scary man who supposedly comes at Christmas to carry naughty children away. Under Papa Doc, the *Tonton Macoutes* were well-armed policemen who beat, imprisoned, and even murdered Haitians believed to be enemies of the Duvaliers.

Papa Doc did not allow anyone to criticize his policies. He wrote a new constitution for Haiti in 1964 in which he declared himself president for life. He did not allow newspapers, television announcers, or radio shows to say anything bad about him, his family, or his government. If they did, they were closed down. In 1963 and again in 1964 groups of his enemies tried to over-throw Papa Doc. Both times they failed. Many Haitians fled their country, most to live in Florida or New York. Some of these refugees hoped to invade Haiti and overthrow the Duvalier regime. One such attempt took place in 1967. It, too, failed. Papa Doc had absolute control over his country.

Dr. Francois Duvalier, "Papa Doc,"
being sworn in as Haiti's
thirty-fourth president in 1957

Baby Doc

In 1971, Papa Doc died. He had planned for his son to succeed him, but not that soon. The constitution stated that the president had to be twenty years old, but Jean-Claude Duvalier was only nineteen. The Haitian legislature, a group loyal to Papa Doc, declared that Jean-Claude was really twenty-one. At nineteen he became president. His nickname was "Baby Doc."

Baby Doc was not as violent and scary as his father had been. He did not use the Tonton Macoutes to terrorize people, but he did use them as armed guards for himself, his family, and the palace. Baby Doc enjoyed living in luxury. Besides the palace, he owned a seaside villa, a ranch, and a mountain hideaway. He liked to sail with friends on his yacht. As long as he could enjoy a wealthy lifestyle, Baby Doc seemed willing to allow his people a bit more freedom than his father had allowed them.

Freedom of this sort did not mean health and employment for the masses of Haitians, however. Thousands of people each year continued to flee to the United States in the hope that they would be allowed to live and work in that country. Other Haitians—especially newspaper journalists and Roman Catholic priests—became increasingly critical of Baby Doc's government. Although Baby Doc borrowed millions of dollars from the United States and other foreign countries, the money did not go to projects to help the people of Haiti. Often it went into the private bank accounts of Baby Doc and his friends.

By the 1980s so many people were criticizing Baby Doc that he tried to shut off the opposition. In the fall of 1980, Baby Doc had one hundred journalists who opposed him thrown in jail. A newspaper editor who escaped, Pierre Clitendre, claimed that "everyone who could speak out has been taken." In March 1983, Pope John Paul II visited Haiti. He spent ten hours in Port-au-

Prince and gave his support to the Roman Catholic priests who opposed the Duvaliers. The Pope declared, "Things must change. . . . The poor of every kind must be able to hope again." Baby Doc refused to allow newspapers to print the Pope's speech.

Many Haitians were also unhappy about Baby Doc's marriage. His wife, Michele, was a light-skinned mulatto. It seemed to some that Duvalier was bringing the élite back to power. Papa Doc had done many bad things, but at least he had given blacks central positions in his government. But Michele Duvalier spent money lavishly and went on shopping sprees in Paris and New York. She did not seem to realize the poverty in her nation.

In July 1985, Baby Doc held an election to demonstrate that he was the people's choice for president. The election was rigged; Baby Doc got 99 percent of the vote. In the late fall there were antigovernment protests in Gonaïves and Cap Haïtien. Then, in January 1986, the United States threatened to cut back aid to Haiti because the Duvalier government did not meet minimal standards of freedom and human decency.

By February, opposition to Baby Doc was so strong that he knew he had to give up the presidency. He left Haiti in the middle of the night, protected by the United States. A military junta under the leadership of Lieutenant General Henri Namphy took control of the country. The junta promised elections, free speech, jobs, and education.

Haitians were jubilant. The dictators were gone. Many people who had emigrated to the United States returned to their homeland. At long last Haiti could be free of dictators. However, the Duvaliers had been in power for so long that it was difficult for Haiti to adjust to a new form of government. So many people were illiterate that it was difficult to hold free elections.

The rule of the Duvaliers has ended, but Haiti remains the poorest nation in the Western Hemisphere. Most of Haiti's

Jean-Claude Duvalier, "Baby Doc,"
with Michele Bennette,
soon before their marriage in 1980

people cannot read or write, do not have jobs, suffer from malnutrition, and do not have enough to feed their families. The average life expectancy for a Haitian is forty-five—nearly thirty years shorter than that of U.S. citizens.

However, Baby Doc Duvalier and his father, Papa Doc, did not create the poverty of Haiti all by themselves. Although they did little to improve conditions, the Duvaliers cannot be held solely responsible for the poverty and destitution of modern Haiti. The Duvaliers are only the most recent in a long series of rulers who have wielded great power in Haiti without bringing about any positive changes for most of the people.

Dictatorship and racism are modern Haiti's legacy from the "glorious years" of the sugar planters as well as from the Duvaliers. Dictatorship and racism have weaved in and out of Haiti's history for the past three hundred years. These two forces have effectively stunted the economy, impoverished the land, and repeatedly dashed the hopes of Haiti's people.

Fortunately, there are also more positive forces that have operated throughout Haiti's history. Haitians may have a long history of dictatorship, but they are also proud that they were the second nation in the Western Hemisphere to win independence from Europe. Haitians have a rich cultural heritage. Their art, music, and religion provide colorful and joyous ways of dealing with daily strife. Haitians have kept many of the customs of the numerous African tribes of their ancestors. They have also borrowed from French, Spanish, and Roman Catholic traditions. The combination is a philosophy of life that is happy, positive, and hopeful. In a land where most people cannot find work, a familiar Haitian proverb goes like this: "If work were such a good thing, the rich would have grabbed it all."

Whatever government leads Haiti into the twenty-first century will have to tackle many problems. The biggest challenge will be to solve the problems without taking away the people's freedom to criticize the government's solutions. The overthrow of the Duvaliers was extremely popular and gave Haitians a sense of pride and control. To be successful Haiti's new government must capitalize on the positive energy that has been unleashed in Haiti. Then Haiti will be able to build a good future based on the positive things in its past.

affranchis (aff ran CHEE)—free black people in Haiti during colonial times.

boucan (boo CAN)—a form of dried beef popular in the West Indies during the seventeenth and eighteenth centuries.

buccaneers—French settlers who killed cows and pigs and turned the meat into *boucan*; because they also attacked Spanish ships, the name is synonymous with pirates.

centime (sahn TEEM)—a Haitian unit of money equal to 1/100th of a gourde.

Code Noir (code NWAR)—a set of laws governing the practice of slavery in the French colonies, developed during the reign of Louis XIV in 1685.

corvée (cor VAY)—a work party organized by Haitian dictators against the will of the workers; used to build roads, bridges, and the like.

coumbite (come BEET)—an informal group of Haitians joined together to help friends and neighbors with projects such as building a barn, repairing a roof, and so on.

Creole (KREE ole)—a language made of a mixture of French, Spanish, and African words, spoken by most Haitians.

crop—slave name for the season when sugar cane was harvested.

élite (ay LEET)—the group of people who believe themselves to be the top layer of society.

gens de couleur (jon duh coo LURE)—light-skinned colonial Haitians with black ancestry who were granted a few political rights during slave times.

gourde (goorde)—the basic unit of money used in Haiti.

houngan (hoo GAN)—chief male voodoo priest.

hounsi basale (hoon see bay SALE)—the youngest assistant priests, either male or female.

hounsi kanzo (hoon see CAN so)—assistant priest in training to become a houngan.

loa—a voodoo god.

mambo—a voodoo priestess.

oungan (oon GAN)—see *houngan*.

out of crop—slave term for the season when the sugar crop was planted.

pase poul (pays pool)—a voodoo medical cure in which an oungan passes a chicken over the body of a sick person.

petits blancs (petty BLONK)—whites in colonial Haiti who did not own large pieces of property.

plaçage (plah SAHJ)—an unofficial wedding that takes place without a priest in attendance.

Tonton Macoutes (tone tone ma KOOT)—the powerful secret police used by the Duvaliers to stay in power.

voodoo (also *voudon* or *voudou*)—a religion and art of healing practiced in Haiti, sometimes referred to as black magic.

INDEX